BFA

"Beauty for Ashes"

STEPHNEY PALMER

ISBN 979-8-89243-113-2 (paperback)
ISBN 979-8-89243-114-9 (digital)

Christian Faith Publishing
832 Park Avenue
Meadville, PA 16335
www.christianfaithpublishing.com

Printed in the United States of America

GIVING THANKS

In the morning, when I am blessed to wake to see another day, sometimes the cares of life cause me, if I am not careful, to forget to give thanks for God's grace and mercy for keeping me through the night. If I do not begin my day with a prayer, asking God to lead and direct me through my day, nothing seems to be right. Giving thanks means that I am making God a priority in my life. By making Him a priority, I allow the Holy Spirit to take full control of my day. Doing this one act of thanksgiving in the morning is a start to a productive day.

Let the morning bring me word of Your unfailing love, for I have put my trust in you. Show me the way I should go, for to You entrust my life. (Psalm 143:8)

Through the Lord's mercies we are not consumed, because His compassions fail not. They are new every morning; great is Your faithfulness. (Lamentations 3:22–23)

PRAYER

Throughout my life, I have known to pray. Prayer for me was something I had to do daily. I cannot remember a day that I did not pray, even when I didn't know if it was effective. The older I got, the more I realized that prayers work and change situations. In the Bible, through the Old and New Testaments, there are stories of how the saints prayed, and God delivered. When Job lost everything, prayer was part of his healing, and God blessed his latter days more than his beginning.

I have experienced the power of prayer repeatedly in my life. If we continue to pray and trust God, He is faithful to deliver. There was a time in my life when I had to have surgery. I was terrified. I love the Lord and believe that He would bring me through, and I knew my church family was praying; however, if I am being honest, although I had faith, I was so nervous, to say the least. I went into prayer, asking God to bring me through, and He did.

The effectual fervent prayer of a righteous man availed much. (James 5:16)

Pray without ceasing. (1 Thessalonians 5:17)

THE HOLY SPIRIT

I must admit that when I became a Christian, I did not truly understand the Holy Trinity. If truth be told, I could not wrap my brain around God in three persons. When someone asked me to explain, I tried with every effort I could muster to make it make sense to them and to myself. As I grew in my faith with much studying of God's word, I asked the Lord to help me understand. It was not until He guided me that I began having conversations with the Holy Spirit daily. I learned that He is a part of the Godhead (Father, Son, Holy Spirit). After learning that the Holy

Spirit lives within me, I learned to surrender my all to Him.

The Holy Spirit is there to guide us through every step of our life. He leads me, directs me, and talks with me through songs, prayers, signs, or just someone saying the right things at the right time. If you are a Christian and have not developed a relationship with the Holy Spirit, ask God to make Himself available in your life. If you are not a Christian, invite the Holy Trinity in your life today. You will be glad you did. If you pray this simple prayer, God is waiting to welcome you with open arms. The Bible tells us that the angels in heaven rejoice over one soul that comes home.

> Lord, I am a sinner. I
> repent of my sins. I believe
> that Jesus Christ is the son of
> God Who died and rose on

the third day. I accept You as Lord and savior. Come into my life. *Amen.*

BROKEN HEART

If you have not been brokenhearted, give it time. Throughout my life, I have been brokenhearted on more than one account—brokenhearted from family, friends, children, coworkers, relationships, and so on. Does this mean that I give up on life, friends, and family? No. If anything, I learn and grow strength from each one.

I recall a heartbreak like it was yesterday. He was my first love. Your first love shouldn't break your heart, right? Not so much. I was heartbroken for what seemed like forever, but I got over it eventually. The Bible teaches us that God heals the brokenhearted and binds up their wounds. He wants us to lean on Him and believe that He can bring us through situations, and He will teach us how to handle them as they arise.

> God heal the brokenhearted and bind up their wounds. (Psalm 147:3)

RESTORE

How do you restore something that has shattered to the point that you don't even think it's restorable? How do you restore a broken heart, a relationship with family, spouse, or friendship? Where do you even start? How do you restore when you are so angry and bitter that you can't even see the forest from the trees? I never knew the importance of the word *restore* until I was faced with a situation in which I had to decide if I wanted restoration. I learned that changes had to be made internally and externally, beginning with your mind, body, soul, and spirit. It's letting go of hurts (past, present, and future) that may occur during the process. This is not an overnight process, and the enemy is lurking around, trying to instill negative thoughts (it's not going to work; you're wasting your time) and laugh. When these thoughts come—and they will—get into the word of God and see what He says about restoration. He will give you peace on your journey. Don't lose heart. Stay with God.

> Resist the devil and he will flee from you. (James 4:7)

> For I will restore health to you and heal you of your wounds; says the Lord. (Jeremiah 30:17)

So, I will restore to you the years that the swarming locust has eaten, the crawling locust and the chewing locust my great army which I sent among you. (Joel 2:25)

GRATEFULNESS

I have so much to be grateful for—my family, my job, my neighbors, my life, my church, and my good friends. I could go on and on, but I would not have enough ink or paper. God has been so good to me in every situation and area of my life. He has been there in the bad times and in the good times.

And He reigns down His grace and mercy each day. He is ever present with me. I can call on Him in the morning, noon, or night. He has never failed me or left me alone, and when I feel like He is not with me, I call upon the name of Jesus, and I feel His peace that surpasses all understanding.

Today, I sat on the beach. I took a brisk walk, taking in the beauty of the morning, feeling the breeze on my face, and thanking God for another day.

He did not have to give this day to me, and it is not because I have been so good but because He is excellent. So many did not wake up on this day to see what I saw, so I am grateful for this gift of life. My prayer today, Lord, is that I may never be ungrateful, but I give You thanks in all things. I will praise You on this day on purpose, for this is the will of God for my life.

Today, take a walk, spend some time in God's presence, and bask in the beauty of His splendor.

The Bible tells us that "morning by morning new mercies I see. All I have need of His

hands have provided. Great is they faithfulness Lord unto me" (Lamentations 3:22–23).

I will bless the Lord
at all times His praise shall
continually be in my mouth.
(Psalm 34:1)

GIVING

If we must be honest, isn't it hard sometimes to give an offering or pay our tithes, especially when you look at what you pay out and then what you have in your hands? The math just does not add up. You know the saying, "Rob Peter to pay Paul"? That saying has rung true to many people. If you have not, God bless you. I remember a time when I "robbed Peter to pay Paul." I was so far in an overdraft that it became my new "normal." It was so bad that I went to the bank one evening after I checked my account, and it was five hundred dollars in the negative. I visited the bank and sat in the parking lot after it was closed. I sobbed and apologized to the bank for always being short. It was a hard time in my life. I did not know where I was going to get the next meal to feed my family, and I was too proud to ask for help. I kept smiling, putting my best face forward. Through it all, I believed that the God of all grace would come through for me.

Shortly after going to the bank to make my big apology, I went to the park on a lunch break. As I sat there under a tree with my windows down in front of a fence, talking to Jesus, crying, pleading, asking Him to help me and lead me because I had nowhere to turn. At that very moment, the presence of God came and sat on the fence. I felt Him as clearly as I felt the wind on my face that afternoon. From that moment until today, God has not left me nor forsaken me.

No matter what may come my way, I know He is only a prayer away. I implore you to trust God. He wants us to come to Him. He wants to give us His blessings. There were times when I didn't have it to pay my tithes, but I found a way. God loves us. If we take care of God's business, He will take care of our business. Give not only in tithes and offerings but also in your time. Give from a cheerful heart and prove Him.

> So let each individual give as he desires in his heart, not grudgingly or of necessity. For God loves a cheerful giver. And God can make all grace abound toward you, that you always having all sufficiency in all things may have an abundance for every good work. (2 Corinthians 9:7).

KINDNESS

Kindness—such a powerful word. Have you ever done something for someone just because? How did it make you feel? Did you feel like this is something you could do more often? Showing kindness doesn't have to cost a thing. One of my greatest satisfactions is doing something kind for others. My daughter told me that I am a "giver." If I have guest(s) at my home (unexpectedly) and have nothing to offer them (to eat or a token to take with them), I feel as if I did not show kindness. This may sound like a craze, but as a person who loves to give to others, this is a great deal. I am reminded that kindness is not about how much you can prepare or give. Sometimes, it's just a kind word, gesture, compliment, a hug, or a smile. These acts of kindness can go a long way.

I challenge you today to show kindness for seven days to a family member, a coworker, a friend, or even a stranger. Jot down what you did. At the end of seven days, think about how each act of kindness changed you and how it made you feel. When Jesus walked the earth, He went around doing good—healing the sick, cleansing the leper, opening blinded eyes, casting out spirits, and saving souls. Jesus showed kindness even to the cross. Remember, He told one of the men who was being crucified that on that day he will be with Him in paradise. Show kindness. It will elevate you to a new level.

Be kind and compassionate to one another, forgiving each other, just as Christ God forgave us. (Ephesians 4:32)

But love your enemies, and do good, and lend, expecting nothing in return, and your reward will be great, and you will be sons of the Most High, for He is kind to the ungrateful and the evil. (Luke 6:35)

FAMILY TIES

Our family has seen its share of heartaches, tears, ups and downs, loss, and gains. We have been mad at each other and even gone weeks, months, and even years without speaking. Despite all these setbacks, we always find ourselves back together. Family will not always agree, but the most important thing is that we remain a family.

Sometimes, you must recognize that your family does not always have to be blood ties. Sometimes it is that foster parents or a neighbor who takes you in and ensures you have all that you need. It could be a church member or even a friend. Family ties, regardless of who you call mom, dad, sister, or brother, are important and should be honored.

As we start each day, let us remember the importance of family. Pray that whatever may happen in life, remain close to one another. Remain strong and forgive. So many are not fortunate to have a family. Do not take this blessed gift for granted.

> But those who won't care for their relatives, especially those in their own household, have denied the true faith. Such people are worse than unbelievers. (1 Timothy 5:8)

COMFORT

What is comfort to you? Is it financial stability, having a good job, living comfortably, or having many friends? All of these could bring comfort, but as you acquire these things, remember God, Who makes all things possible. With Him, I have everything I need. I know I could not live a comfortable life if He did not lead and direct my life.

Yea, though I walk through the valley of the shadow of death I will fear no evil. For thou art with me thy rod and thy staff they comfort me. (Psalm 23:4)

All praise to God, the Father of our Lord Jesus Christ. God our merciful Father and the source of all comfort; He comforts us in all our troubles so that we can comfort others. When they are troubled, we will be able to give them the same comfort God has given us. (2 Corinthians 1:3–4 NLT)

PROSPERITY

Everyone wants to have some level of prosperity. Either winning the lottery, working hard, saving aggressively, being able to buy a fancy car, having good friends, or making a six-figure income. Regardless of how it is accomplished, prosperity can be all those things and more; it is something most would love to have or dream of having. I believe that prosperity is beyond material treasures. What is prosperity, really?

Prosperity is defined as "the state of being prosperous" (Google). Prosperity can be being kind to others, helping someone in need, and being prosperous in the Word of God by gaining wisdom, knowledge, and understanding. The Bible tells us in 3 John verse 2, "Beloved, I pray that you may prosper in all things and be in health, just as your soul prospers." So you see, God wants us to prosper in more ways than just material living. Let our soul, health, body, mind, and spirit prosper as God intended.

SPENDING TIME WITH GOD

Let's admit, unless you purpose in your mind and set time apart to spend with God, the enemy will let so many distractions in your way that you go through the day without even thinking about God.

Spending time with God is more than just going to church on Sunday; it's more than just reading the Bible, and it's more than just saying, "I'm a Christian." Spending time with God means that you must purpose in your heart to put time aside for you and Him. It means having a prayer life; it means spending time fasting and developing a personal relationship with Him.

As you spend time with Him, you will start hearing His voice. He will converse with you through street signs, music/songs, other people, dreams, and His Word. One of the most effective ways to spend time with God is to speak to Him, and He will listen, and then He speaks, and you listen. The Bible tells us that His sheep know His voice. If we study His Word, we will get a better understanding of Who God is—Who the Holy Trinity is. Purpose in your heart to spend time with God. Pray and ask Him to help you to make room for Him. Draw near to God, and He will draw near to you. God really loves you and wants the best for you.

Draw near to God and
He will draw near to you.

Cleanse your hands, you sin-
ners; and purify your hearts,
you double-minded. (James
4:8)

FASTING

What does fasting mean to you? Is fasting effective? Do you see the results of fasting? Does God really demonstrate Himself through fasting? Does what you fast for really comes to pass? The answer for me is *yes*. Your answer may not come in the form that you would like it to or the way you prayed for it, and it may not come when you want it, but the answer will come and be better than you ever imagined.

The Bible tells us that "certain things that we ask of God these kinds do not go out except by prayer and fasting" (Matthew

17:21). Develop a fasting life and watch God work in your situations. For me, when I fast and pray, I see God at work. Not only does He answer my prayer, but He also gives me more than I could imagine. Take note that when you are fasting, it is not for you to announce on the rooftop. That is your time to spend with God in prayer, reading, and meditating on His Word.

FOCUS

It is so hard to stay focused on the things of God. From the moment I open my eyes, my mind is in so many places (work, laundry, dinner, bills, just to name a few). Before my feet touched the floor, it felt like I have enough thoughts in those few minutes to last the rest of the day. I am learning to keep my mind focused on Christ and on the things that are positive, healthy, peaceful, and joyful. When my mind is on these things, it keeps the stressors away.

Finally, brothers, whatever is true, honorable, just, pure, lovely, commendable, if there is any excellence; if there is anything worthy of praise, think about these things. (Philippians 4:8)

Look straight ahead and fix your eyes on what lies before you. (Proverbs 4:25 NLT)

Set your mind on things that are above, not on things that are on earth. (Colossians 3:2)

Be sober minded; be watchful. Your adversary the devil prowls around like a

roaring lion, seeking someone to devour. (1 Peter 5:8)

But his delight is in the
law of the Lord and on His
law, He meditates day and
night. (Psalm 1:2)

RECONCILIATION

The Oxford Language defines *reconciliation* as the restoration of friendly relationships. Do you have friends, family, or neighbors with whom you would like to reconcile? Those who hurt you. What about those who hurt you and want to make it right with you, but your heart is in such a bad place that you would not consider the idea of speaking to them, let alone accepting their friendship again? Some would tell you not to do it—to stay angry. What about the ones who say, "I forgive, but I don't have anything to say to that person"? I believe that reconciliation and forgiveness go hand in hand.

Joseph embraced his brothers and reconciled their relationship (Genesis 45:15). Jesus was reconciled with Peter after he denied Him three times (John 21:15–17). What about the prodigal son, who returned home to his family, asking his father for forgiveness, and without hesitation, his father welcomed him home, and they reconciled?

Holding on to past hurt and choosing not to forgive and reconcile can rob you of your joy. You may say, "I am fine. I am not mad. I don't need that person," however, each time you think of that person or hear their name or if they cross your path, that old devil brings all that anger back to the surface, putting you ten steps back and showing you that you are still struggling to move forward.

The Bible tells us that if you are presenting a sacrifice at the altar in the Temple and you suddenly remember that someone has something against you, leave your sacrifice there at the altar. Go and be reconciled with that person. Then come and offer your sacrifice to God (Matthew 5:23–24). It is important to God that we follow the Word of God. Be that example for your family and friends, and forgive and reconcile with those who hurt you in love.

FRIENDSHIP

Do you consider yourself a friend? Can someone call you a friend? A friend is someone who, no matter what, can tell you when you are wrong, laugh with you, and cry with you. They are your confidant and are loyal to the end. The time will come when that loyalty will be tested, and without strong faith, once that loyalty is broken, it is hard to rekindle. Jesus is the only one Who can be loyal to the end. It is not only that He keeps your secrets, but He will also be closer than any brother. Jesus loves us so greatly that He died on the cross and rose on the third day so that you and

I may have life and have it more abundantly. God wants us to be friendly to the friendless, love one another, and to treat everyone respectfully. Can you imagine if Jesus stopped being our friend? Where would we be? Praise be to God that Jesus is that friend Who sticks closer than a brother.

A man who has friends
must himself be friendly.
But there is a friend who
stick closer than a brother.
(Proverb 18:24)

PEACE

The songwriter says, "Peace! Peace! Wonderful peace coming down from the Father above. Sweep over my spirit forever I pray." What a joy it is to have peace! Not just any peace but the peace of God that surpasses all understanding. I can provide numerous examples of when I am going through situations, and with just a quick prayer asking God to give me peace, before I know it, I am calmed. Peace just comes over me. God does not want us to worry or have anxiety and sleepless nights. No, He wants us to have His peace, joy, wisdom, and understanding. There is nothing worth our peace. Trust in God that He will give you peace.

Peace be within you.
(Psalm 122:8)

DEPRESSION

There are so many things going on in the world today that cause people to be depressed. The economy being at an all-time high is one of the biggest culprits. Let's not mention the loss of jobs, companies shutting down, children rebelling against parents, suicide on the rise, mental health issues, and families falling apart, and these are just some of what causes depression. It seems that there is no help in sight. We have a Savior Who we can lean on—a Savior Who knew that we would be just where we are before life began. Despite all that is going on, His grace is sufficient for us. He said to cast all our cares upon Him. He can keep us from falling. The Lord wants to take care of us. He said He would wipe away all our tears.

Let us let go and let God. Today, turn it over to Jesus and SMILE for the rest of the day. Be blessed.

> Why are thou cast down, O my soul? And why are thou disquieted within me? Hope in God: for I shall yet praise Him, who is the health of my countenance, and my God. (Psalm 43:5)

TITHES AND OFFERING

One of the promises that God made to us is through tithing. He said that by tithing, we trust Him to take care of us when we bring "food" in His storehouse. I am a firm believer in paying tithes and offerings. I can affirm that God will take care of you when you take care of His business. Knowing that my tithes and offerings will be going to help someone in need, beautifying God's house, and paying a bill for someone is a blessing and a testament to the church you pay tithes to. Let us practice tithing and offering and watch God pour out His blessing upon us.

The book of Malachi 3:10 says, "Bring all the tithes into the storehouse that there may be food in My house and try Me now in this says the Lord of host if I will not open for you the windows of heaven and pour out blessings that there will not be room enough to receive it." God wants us to trust and have faith in Him, so He gives us this challenge to prove that He is not a man that He should lie. He will return to you and more. Give and watch your blessings pour in.

> Give and you will receive. Your gift will return to you in full, pressed down, shaken together to make room for more, running over and poured into your lap. (Luke 6:38)

CREATE A CLEAN HEART WITHIN ME

What does the Bible mean when it says create a clean heart within me? David asked God to give him a clean heart because of all his mistakes (sins). David trusted God to forgive him. He also asked God not to cast him from His presence. How many times have we done things when God could have cast us from His presence, but because we sincerely asked for His forgiveness and requested a clean heart, He was faithful to grant our request? David knew that if he continued in his sins, he would lose his position as King of Israel.

God said if we ask Him to forgive us sincerely, He will grant our request. Go to Him today and lay all your sins before Him; ask Him to create in you a clean heart.

He will remove our sins
as far as the east is from the
west. (Psalm 103:12)

BE STILL

So many times, we are so busy talking that we miss the messages God has for us. I find that communication with God is a two-way street. We talk; He listens, and we listen while He speaks. Observe that God's voice is best heard in our silence. How often have you heard someone say, "God doesn't want to hear from someone like me," or, "God is mad at me, so there's no need for me to try to hear from Him." These scenarios couldn't be further from the truth. God is waiting at the door of your heart. He wants to impart His wisdom to us. He loves us so much and wants only the best for those who follow His will. Do not ever think that you are too far gone and that God cannot speak to you and turn things around in your life. He is the God of impossibilities. I challenge you today to surrender your all to Him—the good, the bad, and the ugly—and watch as God turns things around for you.

> Be still and know that I
> am God. I will be exalted in
> the heavens and in the earth.
> (Psalm 46:10)

NOTHING IS IMPOSSIBLE

I heard a song that says, "Nothing is impossible when you put your trust in God." The situations, issues, or problems that are happening in our lives can sometimes seem impossible to get over. We even say, "Only God can change it." This might be the truest statement you have ever made. If we hold to God's unchanging hands, He will never leave us nor forsake us. No matter what you are going through, know that God is the alpha and omega—the beginning and the end. He is a rewarder, and He is more than able to sustain you.

Trust in the Lord with all thine heart; and lean not unto thine own understanding. In all thy ways acknowledge Him, and He shall direct thy paths. (Proverb 3:5–6)

But without faith it is impossible to please Him: For He that cometh to God must believe that He is and that He is a rewarder of them that diligently seek Him. (Hebrews 11:6)

DO GOOD TO OTHERS

Why is it so hard for some people to do good for others? On many occasions, I have been told, "Stephney, you are too nice." I want to say, "Isn't that how we are supposed to be?" It can be very hard to be good to those you know more than to those you don't. My mother used to say, "Be good to others, and good will follow you." Some individuals must work hard to be good, and for others, it is easy. Here is a tip: If you are struggling with doing good for others, pray and ask God to show you how to be kind.

Find someone who needs assistance, whether for a ride to the store or something to eat, give an encouraging message, or just listen. You will be surprised at how good you feel afterward. You may say, "Some people don't deserve it." What if God says you didn't deserve it? Today, make a conscious decision to do good for others.

> And do not forget to do
> good and to share with other,
> for with such sacrifices God
> is pleased. (Hebrews 13:16)

REST

What does it mean to rest? Is it after a long day at work or sleeping in? Is it going for a ride or just sitting on the beach? These are all reasons to rest. What did God mean when He said to rest in Him? Jesus is calling us to lay down our problems and cares—those things that so easily beset us. Come to Him and learn from Him. The rest that we seek for ourselves is temporary, but the rest that Jesus Christ the Savior offers is everlasting. Christ wants us to rest in Him. For only in Him will we find true rest.

Come to Me all you who labor and are heavy laden and I will give you rest. (Matthew 11:28)

WORRY

I wonder what I am going to cook for dinner. Did I turn off the stove before leaving home? Does my outfit look presentable? Where are the children? These are just a few of the hundreds of things that go through our minds every day that cause us to worry. Most of the time, when we find the answers, we realize that the worry is for nothing. We are reminded in the Scripture not to worry, so before worrying, remember the words of the Lord and feed upon them, and before you know it, you will turn your worry into dancing.

Be anxious for noth-
ing, but in everything by
prayer and supplication,
with thanksgiving, let your
requests be made known to
God; and the peace of God,
which surpasses all understanding, will guard your
hearts and minds through
Christ Jesus. (Philippians
4:6-7)

FAULT

How are you admitting your faults? Do you justify when you are called out, or do you get upset? What about just admitting that you are at fault? So many times, the same fault(s) that you see in someone are the same fault that you are carrying. Did Jesus teach us that if someone has something against you, go to him and reconcile with him? Yes, He did. We have all sinned and come short of God's glory, so therefore, when someone faults you, find the time and go to the person and make it right. Today, be the "bigger" person. Think about a fault that is long overdue and needs mending. Go to that person and make it right. Free your mind and your spirit.

> He that covers his sins shall not prosper but whoso confesses and forsakes them shall have mercy. (Proverb 28:13)

WAITING ON GOD

Waiting on God for something you prayed for can be a hard task, especially when you want it now. I must admit that even as Christians, you start to wonder where God is and whether He heard your prayers. You want to ask Him if He cares that you are hurting. "I need You now. God, take this pain away, please." As we go through these difficult times, there is comfort in knowing that God is right there in the midst of going through it with us. The enemy's job is to keep us distracted and to dwell on the problem. But God tells us to trust Him and keep our focus on Him. He wants us to "be still."

When we have done all we can humanly, just "stand" and trust God. While you are waiting, ask Him how you can wait on Him. His grace is sufficient. He is enough. He is going to keep you from falling. He loves you. The God of all peace, joy, and happiness will see you through. Wait on Him.

> Wait on the Lord be of
> good courage, and He shall
> strengthen thine heart: Wait,
> I say on the Lord. (Psalm
> 27:14)

HOLD ON TO GOD

In life, we look for different things to hold on to. Sometimes, life throws us a curveball that turns our lives completely around. With each circumstance, there are different things the enemy put our way to hold on to (alcohol, drugs, wrong relationships). These are all temporary fixes that draw our attention from what is more important. Hold on to God because He's unchanging. He will not leave us in times of trouble. He will see us through to the end.

My soul clings to You,
your right hand upholds me.
(Psalm 63:8)

FINANCIAL SECURITY LOST

It seems that, of late, things are getting harder and harder. People are losing their jobs and homes, businesses are shutting down, and financial security is at a loss. It doesn't matter how much you have or don't have; everyone is affected in some way, whether it be financial, emotional, or physical. Troubles in relationships, families, and marriages are at an all-time high because of the strain. It is easier to just give up instead of staying together. Others are left to pick up the pieces of their lives. Christians—yes, Christians—have turned to the world for help instead of turning to the Creator, Who is the Author and the Finisher of our faith. Despite what we are going through, God will be there for us. He will see us through. He wants us to lay our burdens on Him, and He will take care of us.

> Cast your burden on the
> Lord, and He shall sustain
> you; He shall never permit
> the righteous to be moved.
> (Psalm 55:22)

RESIST THE DEVIL

Have you ever been in such a good mood, and the next minute, your mind goes to a bad place? How many times has someone expressed a negative opinion about you, and it just puts you ten steps backward? The enemy has a way of putting a damper on your mood, especially when you are praising or doing a good deed. The enemy is cunning, and he tries his hardest to get you not to do or enjoy the things of God. He would want us to believe that the world's way is better—that good is bad and bad is good.

He will always show you the glamorous and happy beginning, with no problems, but he will never show you the middle or how it all ends when you follow him, which is destruction. Christ came so that we may have life and have it more abundantly. Trust God. He will never lead you astray.

> The thief cometh not, but for to steal, and to kill, and to destroy. I am come that they might have life, and that they might have it more abundantly. (John 10:10)

STRENGTH

Finding the strength to get out of bed some mornings can be a struggle. Finding the strength to take the next step can cause pain. Finding the strength to walk upright can make you mentally, emotionally, and spiritually weak. There are individuals who possess physical strength, but spiritually, they are weak. Some have spiritual strength, but emotionally, they need guidance. The Bible tells us that Jesus's grace is sufficient for us because His strength is made perfect in weakness. We must understand that God is the only one Who can give us the strength we need. God does not want us to fail. He does not want us to come short but to be strong in every area of our lives. For when we are weak, He is strong.

God is our refuge and
strength, a very present help
in trouble. (Psalm 46:1)

"Grace, grace, God's grace. Grace that will pardon and cleanse within. God's grace is greater than all my sins." These are the lyrics to one of my favorite songs. Who can give us grace but God. Christ tells us that His grace is sufficient for thee.

How many of us have a friend(s) who can give us such grace? Let me know when you find that one. Because of His love for us, He gives us grace that we do not deserve.

 Stephney Palmer is the author of *BFA* (*Beauty for Ashes*). She is a mother of three—two daughters and a son. She lives in Florida with her family. Writing has never been her strong point, but when the Holy Spirit spoke to her heart and said to write, imagine her surprise because she had never written anything before, let alone thought of being an author. Her goal for this book is that it will encourage, uplift, and inspire the hearts of readers.